SO-BOJ-997

CARDINAL NEWMAN'S

DREAM OF GERONTIUS

WITH

Introduction and Commentary

FOR USE IN HIGH SCHOOLS, ACADEMIES
AND COLLEGES

BY

JULIUS GLIEBE, O.F.M.

FRANCISCAN FRIARY, OAKLAND, CAL.

*Sometime Professor of Rhetoric in St. Anthony's Seraphic College,
Santa Barbara, Cal.*

NEW YORK

SCHWARTZ, KIRWIN & FAUSS

COLLEGE OF ST. FRANCIS
EDUCATION DEPARTMENT

COPYRIGHT, 1916, BY

SCHWARTZ, KIRWIN & FAUSS

821.8
N553dgl

CONTENTS

56714

. . . For one who speaks in numbers ampler scope
His utterance finds; and conscious of the gain,
Imagination works with bolder hope. . . .

SONNETS,
WORDSWORTH.

INTRODUCTION

History of the Poem. — The year 1865
found John Henry Newman, the author of
The Dream of Gerontius, an old man, living
with his brethren in quiet seclusion in the
Oratory at Birmingham. He was now close
upon his sixty-fourth birthday, and naturally, as the years advanced, began to look
forward with greater frequency to his approaching end. That supreme moment in
every man's life when the soul goes out to
meet its Judge, had been to him at all times
as if a present reality; and now that the
time was very near, as he thought, when he
should pass " from shadows and images
to the truth," that moment became more
than ever the subject of his thoughts and
meditations. In January, 1865, it suddenly
came into his mind to put his thoughts on
death into the form of a dramatic poem; and

having finished writing it — *currente calamo* as it seems — he laid the thing aside not quite satisfied with it.

A few months later it so happened that Newman was asked by Father Henry James Coleridge S. J., editor of *The Month,* for a contribution to that magazine; and having just then nothing theological to offer, he sent the editor a poem, along with the remark that he might do with it what he chose. The poem thus carelessly offered was none other than *The Dream of Gerontius.* It was thankfully welcomed by Father Coleridge, and shortly afterwards made its appearance in two parts in successive numbers of *The Month*.

After the first part appeared in the May number, Newman wrote to his friend, Thomas William Allies: " As to Gerontius, perhaps the second part will be a failure, so be cautious with your criticism." The second part appeared in the subsequent number, and was received with as much enthusiasm and praise as the first. It would seem that the author was urged to make further additions to the poem, for in another letter to Mr. Allies, written not long after, Newman says: "No, I assure you, I have nothing more to produce of Gerontius. I could no more write anything else by willing it, than I could fly." And to the Reverend John Telford he wrote: "You do me too much honor if you think I am to see in a dream everything that is to be seen in the subject dreamed about. I have said what I saw. Various spiritual writers see various aspects of it, and, under their protection and pattern, I have set down the dream as it came before the sleeper. It is not my fault if the sleeper did not dream more. Perhaps something woke him. Dreams are generally fragmentary; I have nothing more to tell."

The Dream was afterwards added to the author's earlier poems, which were published together under the title *Verses on Various Occasions*. Previous to this, however, a separate edition of the poet's masterpiece had been prepared and brought out, which was affectionately inscribed to a departed

friend and brother Oratorian, Father John
Joseph Gordon, as follows: —

> Fratri Desideratissimo
> Joanni Joseph Gordon
> Oratorii S. P. N. Presbytero
> Cujus Anima in Refrigerio.

In die Comm   J. H. N.
Omn. Fid. Def. 1865.

> To my very dear brother, John Joseph Gordon,
>   Priest of the Oratory of St Philip Neri.
> May his soul be in the Place of Refreshment.
>   JOHN HENRY NEWMAN.

All Souls' Day, 1865.

This edition of *The Dream* has since gone
through more than forty-five reprints. It
was translated into French in 1869, and into
German in 1885. Two other events have
contributed to the increased knowledge and
popularity of *The Dream;* it was made the
subject of an inaugural address by the Professor of Poetry at Oxford, Sir Francis
Doyle; and by Sir Edward Elgar, the cele-
brated composer, was worked into an ora-
torio which, since its first appearance in
1900, has received a wide appreciation at
home and abroad at the hands of the best
musical critics.

The Dream has already taken, and holds to-day, as in 1888 William Ewart Gladstone said it would take and hold its position in the literature of the world. With the best contemporary critics we may confidently say that the great Oratorian's poetic master-piece is simply imperishable, and will ever be numbered among the great poems of the world.

The Metre. — The metre in *The Dream* is as highly varied as it is elegantly chosen. There are throughout the poem no less than eight variations of verse and stanza forms. It is interesting and instructive to observe how wonderfully each measure in its turn obeys, as its dictator, the inner thought and sentiment; and in reading the poem, it is im-possible not to be struck with the author's masterliness, which, with apparent ease and consummate grace, blends the two opposing rhythms, phrasal and metrical, into a living harmony.

The most prevalent measure is the Iambic Pentameter, the standard English line for serious poetry. It is used by the two principal actors in the drama, Gerontius and his Guardian Angel. The recitative and explanatory portions are usually blank, and are massed, according to the sense, into paragraphs of unequal length. But as soon as the underlying sentiment becomes more intense and lyrical, the blank verse is straightway abandoned and gives way, following the current of the sense, to a variety of stanzas, the lines of which are variously grouped and interrelated by means of the rhyme, by the interspersion of alternate trimeters or dimeters, and by the use of an Alexandrine or fourteener as conclusion of a period, — thus transfusing the whole with the life-blood of an ever-changing yet delightfully harmonious movement.

Take the closing lines of the poem, the parting words of the Angel Guardian to the Soul, and observe how fittingly they are thrown into a slightly modified form of the Elegiac Stanza. The standard four alternately rhyming iambic pentameters are, by the introduction of an occasional trochee, and by the addition of a rhyming over-syllable in the second and fourth lines, limbered up to a charmingly graceful and easy movement and softened into a tone of ineffable sweetness and tenderness : —

> Softly and gently, dearly ransomed soul,
>   In my most loving arms I now enfold thee,
> And o'er the penal waters, as they roll,
>   I poise thee, and I lower thee, and hold thee.

This is the movement and tone of purest song, and hence too it so readily lends itself to the rhythm of music : —

Fare - well, | but not | for e | ver, bro | ther dear,

Be brave | and pa | tient on | thy bed | of sor | row.

Swift - ly | shall pass | thy night | of tri | al here,

And I | will come | and wake | thee on | the mor | row.

As an illustration of how pliant and varied in pause, accent, and rhyme the standard verse may under a master hand become, we may instance the passage where the dying

Gerontius describes his feelings of fear and dread at his approaching dissolution:—

I can no more, for now it comes again,
That sense of ruin, which is worse than pain,
That masterful negation and collapse
Of all that makes me man; as though I bent
Over the dizzy brink
Of some sheer infinite descent;
Or worse, as though
Down, down for ever I was falling through
The solid framework of created things,
And needs must sink and sink
Into the vast abyss. And, crueller still,
A fierce and restless fright begins to fill
The mansion of my soul. And, worse and worse,
Some bodily form of ill
Floats on the wind, with many a loathsome curse
Tainting the hallowed air, and laughs, and flaps
Its hideous wings,
And makes me wild with horror and dismay.

Observe, first of all, at what irregular intervals the lines are made to rhyme; and next, how the precipitousness of the " sheer infinite descent " and the consequent horror of the " fierce and restless fright " are strikingly brought out by the sudden breaking off of three of the lines, the very reading of which gives one the sense of bending over a dizzy brink and having one's breath suddenly taken away. Two further lines are cut short, indicating Gerontius' pausing in utter dismay at sight of the Evil One, whose loathsome curses and offensive shrieks are onomatopoetically echoed in the two intervening full lines. And how deftly yet how simply the movement is varied! First, it is accelerated by the use of a trochee - ˘ instead of an iamb ˘-, producing a dactylic interweave in the line: —

Ōvĕr thĕ dīzzy̆ brīnk;

next, two lines later, it is suddenly slowed down by a spondee - -, which admirably brings out the feeling of

Dōwn, dōwn for ever falling;

and then it becomes rapid again, even hurried, and breathless, indicating the departing soul's restless fright and anxious trepidation.

It appears then that the poet, while on the whole faithful to the original pattern of iambic pentameters, still moves with the perfect ease and freedom of a master, obeying only the fundamental require-

ments of the underlying thought; and
by thus continually breaking and varying
the structure of the verse, skilfully avoids
the ever present danger of monotony, which
would else naturally arise from five iambic
feet succeeding each other line after line.

Next to the pentameter in prevalence is
the so-called Ballad Measure, consisting of
two iambic tetrameters alternated with two
rhyming iambic trimeters; which measure
is most suitably adopted for the songs of
creation, fall, and redemption sung by the
five Choirs of Angelicals: —

To us | his el | der race | He gave

To bat | tle and | to win,

With - out | the chas | tise - ment | of pain,

With - out | the soil | of sin.

Then there is the Trochaic Measure, used
in the final prayers of Gerontius and his
Assistants, as also in the pleading of the

Angel of the Agony. Gerontius' prayer takes the form of the alternate rhyming Hymn Stanza, technically called the 8s and 7s, the second and fourth lines being one syllable short. Its light and tripping movement suits well with the confident tone of his dying prayer: —

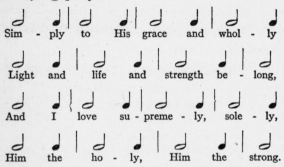

Sim - ply to His grace and whol - ly

Light and life and strength be - long,

And I love su - preme - ly, sole - ly,

Him the ho - ly, Him the strong.

while the solemnity of the reverent and piercingly ardent prayer of the Angel of the Agony aptly registers itself in the trochaic hexameter:—

Je - su, by that shud-dering dread which fell on Thee.

In the Litany of the Saints recited by the Assistants we have a perfect specimen of

interchange and blending of measures. The
Church's solemn prayer is opened in an irregular flow of anxious ejaculatory cries to
Heaven for help in this hour of need. While
for a moment it becomes more even and
quiet, as expressed in the subdued strain of
two iambic lines, it suddenly leaps into the
more rapid anapestic and amphibrach tune,
where with impetuous eagerness God is im-
plored to preserve His servant

> Frŏm thĕ sīns | thăt ăre pāst,
> Frŏm Thy̆ frōwn | ănd Thĭne īre,
> Frŏm thĕ pēr|ĭls ŏf dȳĭng,
> Frŏm ānȳ | cŏmplȳĭng
> Wĭth sīn ŏr | dĕnȳĭng
> Hĭs Gōd, ŏr | rĕlȳĭng
> Ŏn sēlf | ăt thĕ lāst.

Here the first two lines are regular anapestic dimeters, but from the third on each
line snatches in its hurrying course a short
syllable from the next following, thus producing an amphibrach blend; and the anapestic scheme is fully recovered only in the
last line. The Litany then goes on in a
lighter and more confident tone, which is

well expressed in the movement of the
trochee. It appears first in rhymed couplets
of 7s: —

> Bȳ Thȳ | bȋrth ănd | bȳ Thȳ | Crōss
> Rēscŭe | hȋm frŏm | ēndlĕss | lōss ;

and then in rhymed couplets of 11s: —

> Rēscŭe | hȋm, Ŏ | Lōrd, ȋn | thȋs hȋs | ēvȋl | hōur
> Ās ŏf | ōld sŏ | mānȳ | bȳ Thȳ grācĭŏŭs | pōwer.

Finally there is to be noted the measure of
the Demon's Chorus, which is a wonderful
achievement of poetic artistry. The medley
of iambs, trochees, amphimacers, dactyls,
and anapests is completely controlled by the
undertone of phrasal rhythm, which by sudden abrupt breaks and by the congestion
of short syllables operates to produce the effect of a howl of infernal dissonances. The
feet vary in length almost at random from
two to five syllables, yet are so masterfully
held together by a complete scheme of rhyme,
which, though copious and perfect, shoots
to and fro so irregularly that it seems ap-
parently but to serve to heighten the effect
of confusion and disorder. This solitary

note of harmony amid the continued jangle of disharmonies is probably meant by the poet to indicate the one principle upon which these lawless beings are agreed — their inveterate hatred of, and relentless opposition to, God and the human race.

The Flight of the Soul. — *The Dream of Gerontius* is not a theological treatise on the state of the soul after death. But, in spite of what Newman himself has remarked regarding it, — that it is merely a fragment, — in the sense, viz., that the sleeper did not see *all* that was to be seen in that new and undiscovered country, it must nevertheless be admitted that the poem as a whole presents so complete a view of one phase at least of the soul's existence, that it is difficult to see how even formal theology could tell us more of that wonderful flight of the soul from earth to purgatory. This central idea and theme of the poem is beautifully elaborated in seven parts, which are chronologically so closely linked together that they have simply been called paragraphs.

The first of these paragraphs, which serves as an introduction, describes the latter part of that dread hour, the *novissima hora* of this life, the hour of immediate preparation for the Soul's appearance before its Judge. The remaining six paragraphs, which tell the Soul's history in another land, can hardly be said to have any chronology at all,

> For spirits and men by different standards mete
> The less and greater in the flow of time;

and all the Soul's experience, from the instant it leaves the body to its final immersion in the lake, covers a space less than a million-million-millionth part of a moment. Yet in this infinitesimal fraction of a moment we have compressed by a master theologian the vast and complicated history of God's dealings with His creatures.

The Line of Argument. — Following the divisions made by the author himself, we may now attempt a brief characterization of the various parts and point out the leading ideas employed in each paragraph.

Paragraph I. — The prevailing tone of this part is one of deep sorrow and intense pain, yet tempered withal by Christian resignation and confidence in God's abiding love. Gerontius, fortified by the rites of Holy Church, and strengthened by the Bread of the Strong, lies calm and recollected on his death-bed ready to die. But as he hears death knocking its dire summons at his door, he is seized with a sudden terror by which he is driven to invoke the powerful names of Jesus and Mary. The little time that still remains he uses well in making acts of faith, hope, contrition, and love; and then unreservedly surrenders himself into the hands of God.

His account of the awful agony is constantly interspersed by short ejaculatory prayers; and though he instinctively flinches from that " sense of ruin which is worse than pain," he is yet powerfully assisted and buoyed up by the prayers of his friends who presently begin with the attending priest to say the Litany, asking all the Saints of God to intercede for him, and imploring God

Himself to deliver him from the danger of a final fall, and to save him by the merits of Christ. With the words of the expiring Saviour on his lips, Gerontius dies, answering the call of the Master, just at the moment when the priest, in the name of God, bids the Soul go forth on its journey from this world.

Paragraph II. — The final struggle over, Gerontius goes to sleep — the sleep of death, and in the same moment awakens in another world, refreshed by a sense of inexpressible lightness and freedom. But the Soul being deprived of its body, through which on earth it held communion with the outer world, is now thrown entirely upon itself; and, being in a state of separation not originally intended, feels its solitariness out in the deep stillness despite the " sweet soothing rest " of eternity. For a moment it is perplexed in its new surroundings; lodged, as it were, in the rent of the veil that divides this life from the next, it feels itself neither here nor there; from the one side it hears but faint echoes of earthly voices, and on the other it has before it the infinite stretch of the undiscovered country. And as it is borne forward on its way, traversing it knows not whether infinity of space multiplied, or infinitesimalness of space divided, it is suddenly arrested by the Angel's song, in which he tells in heart-subduing melodies the varied history of his client: his high destiny, his fallen state, his costly repurchase, his dreary life-long fray, and relentless fight with the foe, his wonderful nature — a strange composite of heaven and earth, a nature which the Guardian Angel alone among Angels can comprehend. By the drinking in of this heavenly music the Soul becomes

> So whole of heart, so calm, so self-possessed,
> With such a full content, and with a sense
> So apprehensive and discriminant,
> As no temptation can intoxicate.

Paragraph III. — The Soul now fully at home in the Angel's company, would have nothing but to speak with him for speaking's sake. It raises various questions which are answered and explained by the Angel, who

condescendingly assumes the rôle of interpreter. Two misapprehensions are cleared
up, one regarding the nature of eternity,
where

> . . . intervals in their succession
> Are measured by the living thought alone,
> And time is not a common property;

the other regarding the strange disappear-
ance of its one-time fear and dread of having
to meet the awful Judge.

Paragraph IV. — As the Soul and the Angel approach the judgment court, they hear
the fierce hubbub raised by the demons
prowling about the entrance, who mali-
ciously heap all manner of evil names upon
God and man, and contemptuously cast their
venom of abuse on the Saint who gains
the guerdon which they have forfeited. The
Soul is much surprised at their impotence
to harm; but the Angel explains that even
on earth those fallen ones could show so
majestical only because man had a traitor
nestling close at home — his inborn evil
inclinations.

The state of the disembodied Soul is next
portrayed. Bereft of all the senses, the Soul
now lives in a world of signs and types,
wrapped and swathed around in dreams,

> Dreams that are true, yet enigmatical.

Its longing for one glimpse of the Most Fair,
ere it plunges into the avenging flames of
Purgatory, is neither vain nor rash; yet
that sight will not only gladden but likewise
pierce and burn.

Paragraph V. — While the Angel is making it clear to the Soul by a concrete example
what in its present condition its desire to
see God implies, they enter the House of
Judgment, — of which every smallest por-
tion,

> Cornice, or frieze, or balustrade, or stair,
> The very pavement is made up of life —
> Of holy, blessed, and immortal beings,
> Who hymn their Maker's praise continually.

These Angelicals, formed into choirs, sing
of creation, original justice, the fall and redemption; and tell, as only an Angel's deathless fire, an Angel's reach of thought can

tell, of the infinite display of God's victorious grace, of the triumph God has wrought,

> . . . that He who smote
> In man for man the foe,
> The double agony in man
> For man should undergo.

The Angel further explains the nature of the Soul's approaching agony, when it shall be smitten from the face of the Incarnate God with a double pain —

> The longing for Him when it sees Him not,
> The shame of self at thought of seeing Him,

which will be its " veriest, sharpest purgatory."

Paragraph VI. — They pass the gate and come into the veiled presence of God. Just then come floating up from earth the echoes of voices of interceding friends, while the Angel of Christ's Agony, who " saw the Creator reel amid that solitary fight in the garden shade," pleads with the Judge in a litany calm and sweetly pathetic. The Soul is judged as with the intemperate energy of love it flies to the dear feet of Emmanuel; but before it reaches them it is

seized and scorched by the flame of the
Everlasting Love, consumed yet quickened
by the glance of God. The happy suffering
Soul breathes the touching prayer: —

> Take me away, and in the lowest deep
>   There let me be,
> And there in hope the lone night watches keep
>   Told out for me.

Paragraph VII. — The Angel bears the
Soul away through the gates of the Golden
Prison, out of whose depths the sad yet
hopeful strain of the Psalm is heard:
" Lord, Thou hast been our refuge in every
generation." He lovingly dips his precious
burden in the lake, giving his charge to the
keeping of the Angels of Purgatory; and
hovering over the penal waters which close
in upon the dearly ransomed Soul as it sinks
" deep, deeper into the dim distance," he
speaks his tender parting words:

> Farewell, but not for ever! brother dear,
> Be brave and patient on thy bed of sorrow;
> Swiftly shall pass thy night of trial here,
> And I will come and wake thee on the morrow.

THE DREAM OF GERONTIUS

§ 1

Gerontius

JESU, MARIA — I am near to death,
    And Thou art calling me; I know it now
Not by the token of this faltering breath,
    This chill at heart, this dampness on my
        brow,
(Jesu, have mercy! Mary, pray for me!)   5
    'Tis this new feeling, never felt before,
(Be with me, Lord, in my extremity!)
    That I am going, that I am no more.
'Tis this strange innermost abandonment,
    (Lover of souls! great God! I look to
        Thee,)   10
This emptying out of each constituent
    And natural force, by which I come to be.
Pray for me, O my friends; a visitant
    Is knocking his dire summons at my door,
The like of whom, to scare me and to daunt, 15
    Has never, never come to me before;

'Tis   death, — O   loving   friends,   your
    prayers! — 'tis he! . . .
As though my very being had given way,
    As though I was no more a substance now,
And could fall back on nought to be my stay, 20
    (Help,   loving   Lord!   Thou   my   sole
        Refuge, Thou,)
And turn no whither, but must needs decay
    And drop from out the universal frame
Into that shapeless, scopeless, blank abyss,
    That utter nothingness, of which I came: 25
This is it that has come to pass in me;
    Oh horror! this it is, my dearest, this;
So pray for me, my friends, who have not
    strength to pray.

Assistants

Kyrie eleison, Christe eleison, Kyrie eleison.
Holy Mary, pray for him.   30
All holy Angels, pray for him.
Choirs of the righteous, pray for him.
Holy Abraham, pray for him.
St. John Baptist, St. Joseph, pray for him.
St. Peter, St. Paul, St. Andrew, St. John, 35
All Apostles, all Evangelists, pray for him.

All holy Disciples of the Lord, pray for him.
All holy Innocents, pray for him.
All holy Martyrs, all holy Confessors,
All holy Hermits, all holy Virgins,   40
All ye Saints of God, pray for him.

Gerontius

Rouse thee, my fainting soul, and play the
    man;
  And through such waning span
Of life and thought as still has to be trod,
  Prepare to meet thy God.   45
And while the storm of that bewilderment
  Is for a season spent,
And, ere afresh the ruin on thee fall,
  Use well the interval.

Assistants

Be merciful, be gracious; spare him, Lord.   50
Be merciful, be gracious; Lord, deliver him.
  From the sins that are past;
    From Thy frown and Thine ire;
      From the perils of dying;
      From any complying   55
      With sin, or denying
      His God, or relying

LIBRARY
College of St. Francis
JOLIET, ILL.

56714

On self, at the last;
　From the nethermost fire;
From all that is evil;   60
From power of the devil;
Thy servant deliver,
For once and forever.

By Thy birth, and by Thy Cross,
Rescue him from endless loss;   65
By Thy death and burial,
Save him from a final fall;
By Thy rising from the tomb,
　By Thy mounting up above,
　By the Spirit's gracious love,   70
Save him in the day of doom.

Gerontius

Sanctus fortis, Sanctus Deus,
　De profundis oro te,
Miserere, Judex meus,
　Parce mihi, Domine.   75
Firmly I believe and truly
　God is Three, and God is One;
And I next acknowledge duly
　Manhood taken by the Son.

And I trust and hope most fully   80
    In that Manhood crucified;
And each thought and deed unruly
    Do to death, as He has died.
Simply to His grace and wholly
Light and life and strength belong,   85
And I love, supremely, solely,
    Him the holy, Him the strong.
Sanctus fortis, Sanctus Deus,
    De profundis oro te,
Miserere, Judex meus,   90
    Parce mihi, Domine.
And I hold in veneration,
    For the love of Him alone,
Holy Church, as His creation,
    And her teachings, as His own. 95
And I take with joy whatever
    Now besets me, pain or fear,
And with a strong will I sever
    All the ties which bind me here.
Adoration aye be given,   100
    With and through the angelic
      host,
To the God of earth and heaven,
    Father, Son, and Holy Ghost.

Sanctus fortis, Sanctus Deus,
De profundis oro te,   105
Miserere, Judex meus,
Mortis in discrimine.

I can no more; for now it comes again,
That sense of ruin, which is worse than pain,
That masterful negation and collapse   110
Of all that makes me man; as though I bent
Over the dizzy brink
Of some sheer infinite descent;
Or worse, as though
Down, down for ever I was falling through 115
The solid framework of created things,
And needs must sink and sink
Into the vast abyss. And, crueller still,
A fierce and restless fright begins to fill
The mansion of my soul. And, worse and
        worse,   120
Some bodily form of ill
Floats on the wind, with many a loathsome
        curse
Tainting the hallowed air, and laughs, and
        flaps
Its hideous wings,
And makes me wild with horror and dismay. 125

O Jesu, help! pray for me, Mary, pray!
Some angel, Jesu! such as came to Thee
In Thine own agony. . . .
Mary, pray for me. Joseph, pray for me.
Mary, pray for me.   130

Assistants

Rescue him, O Lord, in this his evil hour,
As of old so many by Thy gracious power : —
    (Amen.)
Enoch and Elias from the common doom;
    (Amen.)
Noe from the waters in a saving home;
    (Amen.)
Abraham from th' abounding guilt of Hea-
    thenesse; (Amen.)   135
Job from all his multiform and fell distress;
    (Amen.)
Isaac, when his father's knife was raised to
    slay; (Amen.)
Lot from burning Sodom on its judgment
    day; (Amen.)
Moses from the land of bondage and despair;
    (Amen.)
Daniel from the hungry lions in their lair;
    (Amen.)   140

And the Children Three amid the furnace-
      flame; (Amen.)
Chaste Susanna from the slander and the
      shame; (Amen.)
David from Golia and the wrath of Saul;
      (Amen.)
And the two Apostles from their prison-
      thrall; (Amen.)
Thecla from her torments; (Amen.)   145
        — so, to show Thy power,
Rescue this Thy servant in his evil hour.

Gerontius

Novissima hora est; and I fain would sleep.
The pain has wearied me. . . . Into Thy
      hands,
O Lord, into Thy hands . . .

The Priest

Proficiscere, anima Christiana, de hoc
      mundo!   150
Go forth upon thy journey, Christian soul!
Go from this world! Go, in the Name of
      God,
The Omnipotent Father, who created thee!
Go, in the Name of Jesus Christ, our Lord,

Son of the living God, who bled for thee!   155
Go, in the Name of the Holy Spirit, who
Hath been poured out on thee! Go, in the
        name
Of Angels and Archangels; in the name
Of Thrones and Dominations; in the name
Of Princedoms and of Powers; and in the
        name   160
Of Cherubim and Seraphim, go forth!
Go, in the name of Patriarchs and Prophets;
And of Apostles and Evangelists,
Of Martyrs and Confessors; in the name
Of holy Monks and Hermits; in the name   165
Of holy Virgins; and all Saints of God,
Both men and women, go! Go on thy course!
And may thy place to-day be found in peace,
And may thy dwelling be the Holy Mount
Of Sion: — in the name of Christ, our
        Lord.   170

§ 2

Soul of Gerontius

I went to sleep; and now I am refreshed,
A strange refreshment: for I feel in me
An inexpressive lightness, and a sense

Of freedom, as I were at length myself,
And ne'er had been before.　How still it is!
I hear no more the busy beat of time,
No, nor my fluttering breath, nor struggling
　　　　pulse;
Nor does one moment differ from the
　　　next.
I had a dream; yes: — someone softly said
"He's gone"; and then a sigh went round
　　　the room.　　　　　　　　　　　　　10
And then I surely heard a priestly voice
Cry "Subvenite"; and they knelt in prayer.
I seem to hear him still; but thin and low,
And fainter and more faint the accents come,
As at an ever-widening interval.　　　　　15
Ah! whence is this?　What is this severance?
This silence pours a solitariness
Into the very essence of my soul;
And the deep rest, so soothing and so sweet,
Hath something too of sternness and of pain. 20
For it drives back my thoughts upon their
　　　spring
By a strange introversion, and perforce
I now begin to feed upon myself,
Because I have nought else to feed upon.

Am I alive or dead? I am not dead,   25
But in the body still; for I possess
A sort of confidence which clings to me,
That each particular organ holds its place
As heretofore, combining with the rest
Into one symmetry, that wraps me round,   30
And makes me man; and surely I could
     move,
Did I but will it, every part of me.
And yet I cannot to my sense bring home
By very trial, that I have the power.
'Tis strange; I cannot stir a hand or foot, 35
I cannot make my fingers or my lips
By mutual pressure witness each to each,
Nor by the eyelid's instantaneous stroke
Assure myself I have a body still.
Nor do I know my very attitude,   40
Nor if I stand, or lie, or sit, or kneel.

So much I know, not knowing how I know,
That the vast universe, where I have dwelt,
Is quitting me, or I am quitting it.
Or I or it is rushing on the wings   45
Of light or lightning on an onward course,
And we e'en now are million miles apart.

COLLEGE OF ST. FRANCIS
EDUCATION DEPARTMENT

Yet . . . is this peremptory severance
Wrought out in lengthening measurements
     of space
Which grow and multiply by speed and time?   50
Or am I traversing infinity
By endless subdivision, hurrying back
From finite towards infinitesimal,
Thus dying out of the expansed world?

Another marvel: someone has me fast   55
Within his ample palm; 'tis not a grasp
Such as they use on earth, but all around
Over the surface of my subtle being,
As though I were a sphere, and capable
To be accosted thus, a uniform   60
And gentle pressure tells me I am not
Self-moving, but borne forward on my way.
And hark! I hear a singing; yet in sooth
I cannot of that music rightly say
Whether I hear, or touch, or taste the tones.   65
Oh what a heart-subduing melody!

Angel
My work is done,
  My task is o'er,
    And so I come,

Taking it home,   70
For the crown is won,
  Alleluia,
For evermore.

My Father gave
  In charge to me   75
    This child of earth
    E'en from its birth,
To serve and save,
  Alleluia,
And saved is he.   80

This child of clay
  To me was given,
    To rear and train
    By sorrow and pain
In the narrow way,   85
  Alleluia,
From earth to heaven.

Soul

It is a member of that family
Of wondrous beings, who, ere the worlds
        were made,
Millions of ages back, have stood around   90

The throne of God: — he never has known
     sin;
But through those cycles all but infinite,
Has had a strong and pure celestial life,
And bore to gaze on th' unveiled face of God,
And drank from the eternal Fount of truth, 95
And served Him with a keen ecstatic love.
Hark! he begins again.

Angel

O Lord, how wonderful in depth and height,
    But most in man, how wonderful Thou art!
With what a love, what soft persuasive
    might   100
    Victorious o'er the stubborn fleshly heart,
    Thy tale complete of saints Thou dost
        provide,
    To fill the thrones which angels lost
        through pride!

He lay a grovelling babe upon the ground,
    Polluted in the blood of his first sire,   105
With his whole essence shattered and un-
        sound,
    And coiled around his heart a demon dire,

Which was not of his nature, but had skill
To bind and form his opening mind to ill.

Then was I sent from heaven to set right   110
The balance in his soul of truth and sin,
And I have waged a long relentless fight,
    Resolved that death-environed spirit to
        win,
    Which from its fallen state, when all was
        lost,
    Had been repurchased at so dread a cost. 115

Oh, what a shifting parti-colored scene
Of hope and fear, of triumph and dismay,
Of recklessness and penitence, has been
    The history of that dreary, life-long fray!
    And oh, the grace to nerve him and to lead, 120
    How patient, prompt, and lavish at his
        need!

O man, strange composite of heaven and
        earth!
    Majesty dwarfed to baseness! fragrant
        flower
Running to poisonous seed! and seeming
        worth

Cloking corruption! weakness mastering
    power!   125
Who never art so near to crime and shame,
As when thou hast achieved some deed of
    name; —

How should ethereal natures comprehend
    A thing made up of spirit and of clay,
Were we not tasked to nurse it and to tend, 130
    Linked one to one throughout its mortal
       day?
    More than the Seraph in his height of
       place,
    The Angel-guardian knows and loves the
       ransomed race.

Soul

Now know I surely that I am at length
Out of the body; had I part with earth,   135
I never could have drunk those accents in,
And not have worshipped as a god the voice
That was so musical; but now I am
So whole of heart, so calm, so self-possessed,
With such a full content, and with a sense   140
So apprehensive and discriminant,
As no temptation can intoxicate.

Nor have I even terror at the thought
That I am clasped by such a saintliness.

Angel

All praise to Him, at whose sublime decree 145
   The last are first, the first become the last;
By whom the suppliant prisoner is set free,
   By whom proud first-borns from their
      thrones are cast;
   Who raises Mary to be Queen of Heaven,
   While Lucifer is left, condemned and un-
      forgiven.   150

§ 3

Soul

I will address him. Mighty one, my Lord,
My Guardian Spirit, all hail!

Angel

              All hail, my child!
My child and brother, hail! what wouldest
      thou?

Soul

I would have nothing but to speak with thee 5
For speaking's sake. I wish to hold with thee

Conscious communion; though I fain would
    know
A maze of things, were it but meet to ask,
And not a curiousness.

Angel

                    You cannot now
Cherish a wish which ought not to be wished. 10

Soul

Then I will speak.   I ever had believed
That on the moment when the struggling
    soul
Quitted its mortal case, forthwith it fell
Under the awful Presence of its God,
There to be judged and sent to its own place. 15
What lets me now from going to my Lord?

Angel

Thou art not let; but with extremest speed
Art hurrying to the Just and Holy Judge:
For scarcely art thou disembodied yet.
Divide a moment, as men measure time,   20
Into its million-million-millionth part,
Yet even less than that the interval

Since thou didst leave the body; and the
    priest
Cried " Subvenite," and they fell to prayer;
Nay, scarcely yet have they begun to pray. 25
For spirits and men by different standards
    mete
The less and greater in the flow of time.
By sun and moon, primeval ordinances —
By stars which rise and set harmoniously —
By the recurring seasons, and the swing, 30
This way and that, of the suspended rod
Precise and punctual, men divide the hours,
Equal, continuous, for their common use.
Not so with us in the immaterial world;
But intervals in their succession 35
Are measured by the living thought alone,
And grow or wane with its intensity.
And time is not a common property;
But what is long is short, and swift is slow,
And near is distant, as received and grasped 40
By this mind and by that, and every one
Is standard of his own chronology.
And memory lacks its natural resting-points
Of years, and centuries, and periods.
It is thy very energy of thought 45
Which keeps thee from thy God.

Soul

Dear Angel, say,
Why have I now no fear at meeting Him?
Along my earthly life, the thought of death
And judgment was to me most terrible.
I had it aye before me, and I saw   50
The Judge severe e'en in the crucifix.
Now that the hour is come, my fear is fled;
And at this balance of my destiny,
Now close upon me, I can forward look
With a serenest joy.   55

Angel

It is because
Then thou didst fear, that now thou dost not
          fear.
Thou hast forestalled the agony, and so
For thee the bitterness of death is past.
Also, because already in thy soul
The judgment is begun. That day of doom, 60
One and the same for the collected world, —
That solemn consummation for all flesh,
Is, in the case of each, anticipate
Upon his death; and, as the last great day
In the particular judgment is rehearsed,   65

So now, too, ere thou comest to the Throne,
A presage falls upon thee, as a ray
Straight from the Judge, expressive of thy
    lot.
That calm and joy uprising in thy soul
Is first-fruit to thee of thy recompense,   70
And heaven begun.

§ 4

Soul

             But hark! upon my sense
Comes a fierce hubbub, which would make
    me fear
Could I be frighted.

Angel

            We are now arrived
Close on the judgment court; that sullen
    howl   5
Is from the demons who assemble there.
It is the middle region, where of old
Satan appeared among the sons of God,
To cast his jibes and scoffs at holy Job.
So now his legions throng the vestibule,   10
Hungry and wild, to claim their property,
And gather souls for hell. Hist to their cry.

Soul

How sour and how uncouth a dissonance!

Demons

Low-born clods
    Of brute earth   15
        They aspire
To become gods,
    By a new birth,
And an extra grace,
    And a score of merits,   20
        As if aught
Could stand in place
        Of the high thought,
    And the glance of fire
Of the great spirits,   25
The powers blest,
    The lords by right,
    The primal owners,
        Of the proud dwelling
And realm of light, —   30
Dispossessed,
Aside thrust,
        Chucked down
    By the sheer might

Of a despot's will,   35
    Of a tyrant's frown,
   Who after expelling
   Their hosts, gave,
  Triumphant still,
And still unjust,   40
     Each forfeit crown
  To psalm-droners,
  And canting groaners,
   To every slave,
  And pious cheat,   45
    And crawling knave,
Who licked the dust
    Under his feet.

Angel

It is the restless panting of their being;
Like beasts of prey, who, caged within their
    bars,   50
In a deep hideous purring have their life,
And an incessant pacing to and fro.

Demons

The mind bold
  And independent,
   The purpose free,   55

So we are told,
Must not think
        To have the ascendant.
        What's a saint?
One whose breath   60
        Doth the air taint
Before his death;
        A bundle of bones,
Which fools adore,
                Ha! ha!   65
        When life is o'er;
Which rattle and stink,
        E'en in the flesh.
We cry his pardon!
        No flesh hath he;   70
                Ha! ha!
        For it hath died,
        'Tis crucified
        Day by day,
Afresh, afresh,   75
                Ha! ha!
        That holy clay,
                Ha! ha!
This gains guerdon,
        So priestlings prate,   80

    Ha! ha!
Before the Judge,
        And pleads and atones
For spite and grudge,
        And bigot mood,   85
    And envy and hate,
        And greed of blood.

Soul

How impotent they are! and yet on earth
They have repute for wondrous power and
    skill;
And books describe, how that the very face   90
Of the Evil One, if seen, would have a force
Even to freeze the blood, and choke the life
Of him who saw it.

Angel

       In thy trial-state
Thou hadst a traitor nestling close at home,
Connatural, who with the powers of hell   95
Was leagued, and of thy senses kept the keys,
And to that deadliest foe unlocked thy heart.
And therefore is it, in respect to man,
Those fallen ones show so majestical.

But, when some child of grace, angel or
      saint,   100
Pure and upright in his integrity
Of nature, meets the demons on their raid,
They scud away as cowards from the fight.
Nay, oft hath holy hermit in his cell,
Not yet disburdened of mortality,   105
Mocked at their threats and warlike over-
      tures;
Or, dying, when they swarmed, like flies
      around,
Defied them, and departed to his Judge.

Demons

Virtue and vice,
    A knave's pretence,   110
        'Tis all the same;
        Ha! ha!
          Dread of hell-fire,
      Of the venomous flame,
          A coward's plea.   115
Give him his price,
        Saint though he be,
    Ha! ha!
From shrewd good sense

> He 'll slave for hire   120
> Ha! ha!
> And does but aspire
> To the heaven above
> With sordid aim,
> And not from love.   125
> Ha! ha!

Soul

I see not those false spirits; shall I see
My   dearest   Master,   when   I   reach   His
      throne;
Or hear, at least, His awful judgment-word
With personal intonation, as I now   130
Hear thee, not see thee, Angel?   Hitherto
All has been darkness since I left the earth;
Shall I remain thus sight-bereft all through
My penance-time?   If so, how comes it then
That I have hearing still, and taste, and
      touch,   135
Yet not a glimmer of that princely sense
Which binds ideas in one, and makes them
      live?

Angel

Nor touch, nor taste, nor hearing hast thou
      now;

Thou livest in a world of signs and types,
The presentations of most holy truths,   140
Living and strong, which now encompass
    thee.
A disembodied soul, thou hast by right
No converse with aught else beside thyself;
But, lest so stern a solitude should load
And break thy being, in mercy are vouch-
    safed   145
Some lower measures of perception,
Which seem to thee, as though through
    channels brought,
Through ear, or nerves, or palate, which are
    gone.
And thou art wrapped and swathed around
    in dreams,
Dreams that are true, yet enigmatical;   150
For the belongings of thy present state,
Save through such symbols, come not home
    to thee.
And thus thou tell'st of space, and time, and
    size,
Of fragrant, solid, bitter, musical,
Of fire, and of refreshment after fire;   155
As (let me use similitude of earth,

To aid thee in the knowledge thou dost
      ask) —
As ice which blisters may be said to burn.
Nor hast thou now extension, with its parts
Correlative, — long habit cozens thee, —   160
Nor power to move thyself, nor limbs to
      move.
Hast thou not heard of those, who after loss
Of hand or foot, still cried that they had
      pains
In hand or foot, as though they had it still?
So is it now with thee, who hast not lost   165
Thy hand or foot, but all which made up
      man.
So will it be, until the joyous day
Of resurrection, when thou wilt regain
All thou hast lost, new-made and glorified.
How, even now, the consummated Saints   170
See God in heaven, I may not explicate.
Meanwhile, let it suffice thee to possess
Such means of converse as are granted thee,
Though, till that Beatific Vision, thou art
      blind;
For e'en thy purgatory, which comes like fire, 175
Is fire without its light.

Soul

His will be done!
I am not worthy e'er to see again
The face of day; far less His countenance
Who is the very sun. Nathless, in life,
When I looked forward to my purgatory,   180
It ever was my solace to believe
That, ere I plunged amid th' avenging flame,
I had one sight of Him to strengthen me.

Angel

Nor rash nor vain is that presentiment;
Yes, — for one moment thou shalt see thy
        Lord.   185
Thus will it be: what time thou art arraigned
Before the dread tribunal, and thy lot
Is cast forever, should it be to sit
On His right hand among His pure elect,
Then sight, or that which to the soul is sight, 190
As by a lightning-flash, will come to thee,
And thou shalt see, amid the dark profound,
Whom thy soul loveth, and would fain ap-
        proach, —
One moment; but thou knowest not, my
        child,

What thou dost ask: that sight of the Most
    Fair   195
Will gladden thee, but it will pierce thee too.

Soul

Thou speakest darkly, Angel! and an awe
Falls on me, and a fear lest I be rash.

Angel

There was a mortal, who is now above
In the mid glory: he, when near to die,   200
Was given communion with the Crucified, —
Such, that the Master's very wounds were
    stamped
Upon his flesh; and, from the agony
Which thrilled through body and soul in that
    embrace,
Learn that the flame of the Everlasting Love 205
Doth burn ere it transform. . . .

§ 5

    . . . Hark to those sounds!
They come of tender beings angelical,
Least and most childlike of the sons of God.

First Choir of Angelicals

Praise to the Holiest in the height,
   And in the depth be praise: 5
In all His words most wonderful;
   Most sure in all His ways!

To us His elder race He gave
   To battle and to win,
Without the chastisement of pain,   10
   Without the soil of sin.

The younger son He willed to be
   A marvel in his birth:
Spirit and flesh his parents were;
   His home was heaven and earth.   15

The Eternal blessed His child, and armed,
   And sent him hence afar,
To serve as champion in the field
   Of elemental war.

To be His Viceroy in the world   20
   Of matter, and of sense;
Upon the frontier, towards the foe,
   A resolute defence.

Angel

We now have passed the gate, and are within
The House of Judgment; and whereas on
      earth   25
Temples and palaces are formed of parts
Costly and rare, but all material,
So in the world of spirits nought is found,
To mould withal and form into a whole,
But what is immaterial; and thus   30
The smallest portions of this edifice,
Cornice, or frieze, or balustrade, or stair,
The very pavement is made up of life —
Of holy, blessed, and immortal beings,
Who hymn their Maker's praise continually. 35

Second Choir of Angelicals

Praise to the Holiest in the height,
    And in the depth be praise:
In all His words most wonderful;
    Most sure in all His ways!

Woe to thee, man! for he was found   40
    A recreant in the fight;
And lost his heritage of heaven,
    And fellowship with light.

Above him now the angry sky,
    Around, the tempest's din;   45
Who once had Angels for his friends,
    Had but the brutes for kin.

O man! a savage kindred they;
    To flee that monster brood
He scaled the seaside cave, and clomb   50
    The giants of the wood.

With now a fear, and now a hope,
    With aids which chance supplied,
From youth to eld, from sire to son,
    He lived, and toiled, and died.   55

He dreed his penance age by age;
    And step by step began
Slowly to doff his savage garb
    And be again a man.

And quickened by the Almighty's breath, 60
    And chastened by His rod,
And taught by Angel-visitings,
    At length he sought his God;

And learned to call upon His name,
    And in His faith create   65
A household and a fatherland,
    A city and a state.

Glory to Him who from the mire,
  In patient length of days,
Elaborated into life   70
  A people to His praise!

Soul

The sound is like the rushing of the wind —
The summer wind among the lofty pines;
Swelling and dying, echoing round about,
Now here, now distant, wild and beautiful; 75
While, scattered from the branches it has
      stirred,
Descend ecstatic odors.

Third Choir of Angelicals

Praise to the Holiest in the height,
  And in the depth be praise:
In all His words most wonderful;   80
  Most sure in all His ways!

The Angels, as beseemingly
  To spirit-kind was given,
At once were tried and perfected,
  And took their seats in heaven.   85

For them no twilight or eclipse;
  No growth and no decay:

'Twas hopeless, all-ingulfing night,
　　Or beatific day.

But to the younger race there rose   90
　　A hope upon its fall;
And slowly, surely, gracefully,
　　The morning dawned on all.

And ages, opening out, divide
　　The precious and the base,   95
And from the hard and sullen mass
　　Mature the heirs of grace.

O man! albeit the quickening ray,
　　Lit from his second birth,
Makes him at length what once he was,   100
　　And heaven grows out of earth;

Yet still between that earth and heaven —
　　His journey and his goal —
A double agony awaits
　　His body and his soul.   105

A double debt he has to pay —
　　The forfeit of his sins:
The chill of death is past, and now
　　The penance-fire begins.

Glory to Him, who evermore   110
　　By truth and justice reigns;

Who tears the soul from out its case,
And burns away its stains!

Angel

They sing of thy approaching agony,
Which thou so eagerly didst question of: 115
It is the face of the Incarnate God
Shall smite thee with that keen and subtle
pain;
And yet the memory which it leaves will be
A sovereign febrifuge to heal the wound;
And yet withal it will the wound provoke, 120
And aggravate and widen it the more.

Soul

Thou speakest mysteries; still methinks I
know
To disengage the tangle of thy words:
Yet rather would I hear thy angel voice,
Than for myself be thy interpreter. 125

Angel

When then — if such thy lot — thou seest
thy Judge,
The sight of Him will kindle in thy heart
All tender, gracious, reverential thoughts.

Thou wilt be sick with love, and yearn for
    Him,
And feel as though thou couldst but pity
    Him,   130
That one so sweet should e'er have placed
    Himself
At disadvantage such, as to be used
So vilely by a being so vile as thee.
There is a pleading in His pensive eyes
Will pierce thee to the quick, and trouble
    thee.   135
And thou wilt hate and loathe thyself; for,
    though
Now sinless, thou wilt feel that thou hast
    sinned,
As never thou didst feel; and wilt desire
To slink away, and hide thee from His sight:
And yet wilt have a longing aye to dwell   140
Within the beauty of His countenance.
And these two pains, so counter and so
    keen, —
The longing for Him, when thou seest Him
    not;
The shame of self at thought of seeing
    Him, —
Will be thy veriest, sharpest purgatory.   145

Soul

My soul is in my hand: I have no fear, —
In His dear might prepared for weal or woe.
But hark! a grand mysterious harmony:
It floods me like the deep and solemn sound
Of many waters.

Angel

      We have gained the stairs 150
Which rise towards the Presence-chamber;
    there
A band of mighty Angels keep the way
On either side, and hymn the Incarnate God.

Angels of the Sacred Stair

Father, whose goodness none can know, but
    they
    Who see Thee face to face,   155
By man hath come the infinite display
    Of Thy victorious grace;
But fallen man — the creature of a day —
    Skills not that love to trace.
It needs, to tell the triumph Thou hast
    wrought,   160
An Angel's deathless fire, an Angel's reach
    of thought.

It needs that very Angel who with awe,
    Amid the garden shade,
The great Creator in His sickness saw,
    Soothed by a creature's aid,   165
And agonized, as victim of the Law
    Which He Himself had made;
For who can praise Him in His depth and
    height,
But he who saw Him reel amid that solitary
    fight?

Soul

  Hark! for the lintels of the presence-gate 170
Are vibrating and echoing back the strain.

Fourth Choir of Angelicals

Praise to the Holiest in the height,
    And in the depth be praise:
In all His words most wonderful;
    Most sure in all His ways!   175

The foe blasphemed the Holy Lord,
    As if He reckoned ill,
In that He placed His puppet man
    The frontier place to fill.

For even in his best estate,   180
    With amplest gifts endued,

A sorry sentinel was he,
   A being of flesh and blood.

As though a thing, who for his help
   Must needs possess a wife,   185
Could cope with those proud rebel hosts
   Who had angelic life.

And when, by blandishment of Eve,
   That earth-born Adam fell,
He shrieked in triumph, and he cried,   190
   " A sorry sentinel;

" The Maker by His word is bound,
   Escape or cure is none;
He must abandon to his doom,
   And slay His darling son."   195

Angel

And now the threshold, as we traverse it,
Utters aloud its glad responsive chant.

Fifth Choir of Angelicals

Praise to the Holiest in the height,
   And in the depth be praise:
In all His words most wonderful;   200
   Most sure in all His ways!

O loving wisdom of our God!
  When all was sin and shame,
A second Adam to the fight
  And to the rescue came.   205

O wisest love! that flesh and blood
  Which did in Adam fail,
Should strive afresh against the foe,
  Should strive and should prevail.

And that a higher gift than grace   210
  Should flesh and blood refine,
God's Presence and His very Self,
  And Essence all divine.

O generous love! that He who smote
  In man for man the foe,   215
The double agony in man
  For man should undergo;

And in the garden secretly,
  And on the cross on high,
Should teach His brethren and inspire   220
  To suffer and to die.

§ 6
Angel

Thy judgment now is near, for we are come
Into the veiled presence of our God.

Soul

I hear the voices that I left on earth.

Angel

It is the voice of friends around thy bed,
Who say the " Subvenite " with the priest.   5
Hither the echoes come; before the Throne
Stands the great Angel of the Agony,
The same who strengthened Him, what time
      He knelt
Lone in the garden shade, bedewed with
      blood.
That Angel best can plead with Him for all   10
Tormented souls, the dying and the dead.

Angel of the Agony

Jesu! by that shuddering dread which fell on
      Thee;
Jesu! by that cold dismay which sickened
      Thee;
Jesu! by that pang of heart which thrilled in
      Thee;
Jesu! by that mount of sins which crippled
      Thee;   15
Jesu! by that sense of guilt which stifled
      Thee;

Jesu! by that innocence which girdled Thee,
Jesu! by that sanctity which reigned in Thee;
Jesu! by that Godhead which was one with
       Thee;
Jesu! spare these souls which are so dear to
       Thee;
Who in prison, calm and patient, wait for
       Thee;
Hasten, Lord, their hour, and bid them come
       to Thee,
To that glorious Home, where they shall
       ever gaze on Thee.

Soul

I go before my Judge. Ah! . . .

Angel

       . . . Praise to His Name! 25
The eager spirit has darted from my hold,
And, with the intemperate energy of love,
Flies to the dear feet of Emmanuel;
But, ere it reach them, the keen sanctity,
Which with its effluence, like a glory, clothes 30
And circles round the Crucified, has seized,
And scorched, and shrivelled it; and now it
       lies

Passive and still before the awful Throne.
O happy, suffering soul! for it is safe,
Consumed, yet quickened, by the glance of
      God.   35

Soul

Take me away, and in the lowest deep
      There let me be,
And there in hope the lone night-watches
      keep,
      Told out for me.
There, motionless and happy in my pain,   40
      Lone, not forlorn, —
There will I sing my sad perpetual strain,
      Until the morn.
There will I sing, and soothe my stricken
      breast,
      Which ne'er can cease   45
To throb, and pine, and languish, till possest
      Of its Sole Peace.
There will I sing my absent Lord and
      Love: —
      Take me away,
That sooner I may rise, and go above,   50
And see Him in the truth of everlasting day.

§ 7

Angel

Now let the golden prison ope its gates,
Making sweet music, as each fold revolves
Upon its ready hinge.   And ye great powers,
Angels of Purgatory, receive from me
My charge, a precious soul, until the day,   5
When, from all bond and forfeiture released,
I shall reclaim it for the courts of light.

Souls in Purgatory

1. Lord, Thou hast been our refuge: in
   every generation;
2. Before the hills were born, and the
   world was: from age to age Thou art
   God.
3. Bring us not, Lord, very low: for Thou
   hast said, Come back again, ye sons
   of Adam.   10
4. A thousand years before Thine eyes are
   but as yesterday: and as a watch of
   the night which is come and gone.
5. The grass springs up in the morning:
   at evening-tide it shrivels up and
   dies.

6. So we fail in Thine anger: and in Thy
   wrath we are troubled.

7. Thou hast set our sins in Thy sight:
   and our round of days in the light of
   Thy countenance.

8. Come back, O Lord! how long: and be
   entreated for Thy servants. 15

9. In Thy morning we shall be filled with
   Thy mercy: we shall rejoice and be
   in pleasure all our days.

10. We shall be glad according to the days
    of our humiliation: and the years in
    which we have seen evil.

11. Look, O Lord, upon Thy servants and
    on Thy work: and direct their
    children.

12. And let the beauty of the Lord our God
    be upon us; and the work of our
    hands, establish Thou it.

Glory be to the Father, and to the Son: and
   to the Holy Ghost. 20

As it was in the beginning, is now, and ever
   shall be: world without end. Amen.

Angel

Softly and gently, dearly ransomed soul,

In my most loving arms I now enfold
    thee,
And, o'er the penal waters, as they roll,
    I poise thee, and I lower thee, and hold
    thee.   25

And carefully I dip thee in the lake,
    And thou, without a sob or a resistance,
Dost through the flood thy rapid passage
    take,
    Sinking deep, deeper, into the dim
    distance.

Angels, to whom the willing task is given,   30
    Shall tend, and nurse, and lull thee, as
    thou liest;
And masses on the earth, and prayers in
    heaven,
    Shall aid thee at the Throne of the Most
    Highest.

Farewell, but not for ever! brother dear,
    Be brave and patient on thy bed of
    sorrow;   35
Swiftly shall pass thy night of trial here,
    And I will come and wake thee on the
    morrow.

APPRECIATIONS

The Dream is a rare rendering into English verse of that high ritual which, from the deathbed to the Mass of Supplication, encompasses the faithful soul. It pierces, indeed, beyond the veil, but in strict accordance or analogy with what every Catholic holds to be there. Hence we shall interpret its meaning if we liken it, not to Milton, whose supernatural worlds are his peculiar device, founded upon heathen rather than Christian tradition; nor to Dante, who mingles history and landscape from his time and travels in the solemn sweet *Purgatorio* which remains his masterpiece, but to Calderon's *Autos Sacramentales,* at once an allegory and an act of faith. . . . *The Dream* is the answer given at length to *Lead, kindly Light* — a revelation of the Unseen, severe yet tender, demanding an heroic service, but to One who was entirely human; the simple

Christian truth, set in a mystery almost scenic, that it might be the more taking.

WILLIAM BARRY.

The Dream of Gerontius was the true copestone for Newman to cut and lay on the literary and religious work of his whole life. Had Dante himself composed *The Dream* as his elegy on the death of some beloved friend, it would have been universally received as altogether worthy of his superb genius, and it would have been a jewel altogether worthy of his peerless crown. There is nothing of its kind, outside of the *Purgatorio* and the *Paradiso,* at all equal to *The Dream* for solemnizing, ennobling, and sanctifying power. It is a poem that every man should have by heart who has it before him to die.

ALEXANDER WHYTE.

The Dream of Gerontius resembles Dante more than any other poetry written since the great Tuscan's time.

SIR HENRY TAYLOR.

To my mind *The Dream of Gerontius* is the poem of a man to whom the vision of the Christian revelation has at all times been more real, more potent to influence action, and more powerful to preoccupy the imagination than all worldly interests put together.

RICHARD H. HUTTON.

NEWMAN'S poems are not so well known as his prose, but the reader who examines the *Lyra Apostolica* and *Verses on Various Occasions* will find many short poems that stir a religious nature profoundly by their pure and lofty imagination; and future generations may pronounce one of these poems — *The Dream of Gerontius* — to be Newman's most enduring work. . . . Both in style and in thought *The Dream* is a powerful and original poem, and is worthy of attention not only for itself, but, as a modern critic suggests, " as a revelation of that high spiritual purpose which animated Newman's life from beginning to end."

W. J. LONG.

NOTES ON THE DREAM

PARAGRAPH I.

Gerontius. From the Greek γέρων, an old man.

Line 1. Jesu, Maria. The Latin forms for the two sacred names which a Christian invokes most frequently in life, and which now in his last extremity Gerontius instinctively calls upon.

10. Lover of souls! . . . Note the firmness of the ejaculatory prayers interspersed in the dread account of his agony.

11. This emptying out . . . The soul of Gerontius is gradually disengaging itself and receding from the outer senses of the body.

17. your prayers! . . . As one sense after another grows weaker, he begins to feel his loneliness, and asks the prayers of the bystanders.

28. who have not strength to pray . . . In his growing dread of falling out into the great deep, he again begs the prayers of his friends. The urgency of the appeal is emphasized by the addition in the metre of an extra foot.

29. Kyrie Eleison . . . Κύριε ἐλέησον, the Greek for *Lord have mercy.*

42. Rouse thee . . . Having recovered from

the first storm of bewilderment, thanks to the prayers of the bystanders, Gerontius, summoning all his strength, speaks courage to his soul, to prepare to meet his God.

52-63. Interchange and blending of measures. See Introd. p. 12.

72. Sanctus fortis . . . Holy Strong One, Holy God — From the depths I pray to Thee — Be Thou merciful, my Judge — Spare Thou me, O Lord.

77. God is Three and God is One. . . . The mystery of the Blessed Trinity: God is Three in Person, but One in Substance.

94. Holy Church . . . The teaching body established by Christ to be for all times and for all men the oracle of God.

107. Mortis in discrimine . . . In death's critical moment.

108-125. Pliancy of measure illustrated. See Introd. p. 7.

119. Note the significant alliteration in this line.

122. Note the onomatopoetic effect of the hissing words echoing the demons' offensive shrieks.

126. O Jesu, help! . . . Under fire of temptation from the devil, Gerontius, now brought to the last extremity, takes recourse to Jesus, Mary, and Joseph. His weakness is aptly indicated by the stopping short of this line and the irregular flow of the metre in the next.

131. Rescue him, O Lord. . . . Seeing Geron-

NOTES **77**

tius in the throes of his last agony, the bystanders, still following the Church's ritual, confidently ask of God to rescue the dying man, as He had rescued so many of His servants of old.

144. the two Apostles . . . St. Peter and St. Paul.

147. Novissima hora est . . . The last moment is come.

149. into Thy hands . . . The last words of the dying Saviour.

150. Proficiscere, anima Christiana . . . The opening line of the Church's prayer at the moment of the soul's departure. The next line and a half is a translation of it; the solemn prayer then goes on to the end in a beautifully rendered English version.

PARAGRAPH II.

Line 1. I went to sleep . . . The sleep of death.

1-8. How light and buoyant the movement of these lines, the sound answering to the sense!

9. I had a dream . . . The key-note to the poem.

12. Subvenite . . . The opening word of the prayer recited by the priest immediately after the death of Gerontius: Subvenite, Sancti Dei; occurrite, Angeli Domini, Suscipientes animam ejus;

Offerentes eam in conspectu Altissimi: Come to his assistance, ye Saints of God; come forth to meet him, ye Angels of the Lord; Receiving his soul; Offering it in the sight of the Most High.

22. **By a strange introversion** . . . Here on earth the Soul's thoughts were occupied for the most part with things external to itself, and always conditioned by the operations of the various senses; but now, in its state of severance from the senses, living " out of the expansed world," the Soul has " nought to feed upon " but itself, and hence its thoughts are naturally driven back " upon their spring by a strange introversion."

45-46. **Or I or it is rushing** . . . Note the rapid movement of these lines, indicating the swiftness of the Soul's flight.

45-54. An illustration of Newman's perfect mastery over form, which he knows how to bend and shape at will to suit the requirements of the underlying and determining thought. Observe the two sublimities of space, boundless in extent, and endless in divisibility; both majestic in their expression, yet contrasted in their movements: the one grave and measured,

> Wrought out in lengthening measure-
> ments of space,

the other light and tripping,

> By endless subdivision hurrying back.

55. **some one** . . . Gerontius' Angel Guardian. It is Catholic teaching that every man is given at his birth a ministering angel whose office it is to guide and protect his client through life.

66. **Oh what a heart-subduing melody!** . . . The Angel overjoyed at his client's final victory and his own task successfully performed, breaks out into a jubilant song of triumph.

72. **Alleluia** . . . A Hebrew compound word meaning *Praise ye the Lord*.

89. **Of wondrous beings** . . . The nine choirs of Angels.

90. **Millions of ages back** . . . Before the creation of the visible world.

98. **O Lord, how wonderful** . . . The Angel looks serenely back upon the long and arduous struggle of his client, recounts his varied history, of which, having been his constant, lifelong companion, he knows every particular, and gives glory and praise to God, "at whose sublime decree the last are first, the first become the last."

105. **in the blood of his first sire** . . . By the sin of Adam.

107. **a demon dire** . . . Man's proneness to evil resulting from original sin.

115. **at so dread a cost** . . . The life-blood of the Saviour.

122. **O man, strange composite** . . . The greatness and littleness of man are here expressed with

a precision and a boldness of contrast that rival
the excellence, if not the celebrity of Shakespeare's
and Young's parallel passages : —

What a piece of work is man! How noble in
reason! how infinite in faculties! in form, and
moving, how express and admirable! in action, how
like an angel! in apprehension, how like a god!
the beauty of the world! the paragon of animals!
And yet, to me, what is this quintessence of dust?

Hamlet, Act II. Sc. 2.

How poor, how rich, how abject, how august,
How complicate, how wonderful is man!
Distinguished link in being's endless chain;
Midway from nothing to the Deity!
A beam ethereal, sullied and absorpt;
Though sullied and dishonored, still divine!
Dim miniature of greatness absolute;
An heir of glory; a frail child of dust:
Helpless immortal! insect infinite!
A worm! A god!

Night Thoughts. Man.

132. More than the Seraph . . . How beautiful and touching the sympathy of the Angel with
man, his younger brother.

137. as a god . . . The Soul calls the Angel
a god in the unusual sense in which it is sometimes
found in Scripture; e. g. Ps. 81 : 6, John 10 : 34.

142. As no temptation can intoxicate . . .

The Soul can no longer be deceived by sinful allurements.

144. such a saintliness . . . On earth saintliness is sometimes stern and forbidding, and more often inspires awe than confidence.

PARAGRAPH III.

Line 16. What lets me . . . To *let* is to prevent.

24. Subvenite . . . See note on line 12 of paragraph II.

29. rise and set harmoniously . . . That is with perfect regularity.

31. the suspended rod . . . The pendulum.

42. standard of his own chronology . . . Length, swiftness, nearness, and their opposites are all relative ideas, which vary according to the mind's intensity and energy of thought. The mind needs in its judgments no longer to conform itself to external things, but they to the mind. A passage in Dante's *Purgatorio* expresses the same thought : —

So here the ambient air
Weareth that form, which influence of the soul
Imprints on it.

Canto XXV.

53. balance of my destiny . . . Whether saved or lost for all eternity.

63. anticipate . . . An old preterite form for anticipated.

70. first fruit . . . of thy recompense . . . Possibly the reward for his good deeds as done in obedience to the dictate of reason.

PARAGRAPH IV.

Line 12. Hist to their cry . . . As soon as the demons, prowling about the judgment seat, catch sight of the Soul borne hitherward by the Angel, and from its fearless and tranquil manner conclude that it is likely to get from the Judge a favorable sentence, they are suddenly seized anew by envious hate, and break out into a ranting tirade, in which they heap all manner of evil names upon God and man: God they call a despot and a tyrant; man, a low-born clod; the con-templative, a psalm-droner; the preacher, a canting groaner; the doer of the law, a slave; the devout person, a pious cheat; the humble man, a crawling knave.

18. By a new birth . . . That is, by Baptism.

19. an extra grace . . . The grace of Redemp-tion through the Saviour.

23-29. Of the high thought . . . The demons here unwittingly describe the state of the faithful Angels, — the high eminence, from which as rebels they had justly been hurled; but in their vault-ing pride, they stubbornly refuse to acknowledge the justice of their punishment, and would fain still be great spirits, powers blest, lords, primal owners of the realm of light.

56. So we are told . . . The demons are constrained to admit their hopeless state of bondage; and, as if to compensate themselves for the forced admission, fly into a contemptuous rage, casting their venom of abuse upon the Saint who by his loyalty wins the prize which they have lost.

59. What's a Saint? . . . Contrast the picture here given by the demons of man and his varied history, with the picture drawn by the Angel in his song of victory, as remarked upon in note on line 66 of paragraph II. The demons' vision is distorted, and the picture they draw reflects but the black and murky colors of their own utter baseness, and their torn recital of man's laborious upward striving strikes but the notes of sardonic scorn, satanic hate, and wild ghoulish jealousy.

94. Thou hadst a traitor . . . The disordered tendency, called concupiscence, through which man's heart is from his youth up inclined to sin and rebellion.

125. And not from love . . . The demons, unable to deny that the Saint has reached his last end and highest good, mockingly insinuate that after all it was only sordid selfishness that moved him to love and to serve his God.

149. And thou art wrapped and swathed

around in dreams . . . This line gives the clue to the title "Dream." The soul, having passed the threshold of this mortal life, finds that, with the loss of its outer senses, it has lost too its connatural means of converse with the external world. But just as in a dream the mind ranges amid the images of the various impressions received in the waking state, so, in like manner, does the disembodied spirit live, as it were, among its own reminiscences, and more especially among the truths of faith which on earth, albeit they were seen but through a glass darkly, were yet its truest and highest possession: — it is said, now that it has wholly transcended the experiences of sense, in a manner to *dream*

As ice which blisters may be said to burn.

It is this novel and mysterious mode of perceiving things spiritual that gives significance to the title of the poem. It is not simply Newman's habitual caution in dealing with subjects of importance — as Maurice Francis Egan suggests, — that has led him to call the poem a "Dream," as if the author had been unwilling to set forth his thoughts and poetical musings on that solemn moment of death as representing actual facts; nor yet, — as Alexander Whyte seems to hold — the false notion that the Soul on its first entrance into the realm of light should possess a lesser degree of self-consciousness than it had the moment before: but it is rather, as

I venture to think, the fact that Gerontius' Soul, now free and unencumbered, has at last gone out among the immensities, if not straightway to see face to face, at least by a lower measure of perception to DREAM, the realities of that higher world which it has entered.

159. Nor hast thou now extension . . . Extension, being a property of matter in virtue of which the different portions of a material body correspond to the different portions of space, cannot be a property of the soul, which is in its nature a spiritual and an uncompounded being.

167. day of resurrection . . . The day of the Last Judgment, when all men will rise from the dead, the good unto glory, the wicked unto damnation.

174. Beatific Vision . . . The happiness which the Blessed in heaven enjoy by seeing God face to face, and participating in the Divine Nature and in God's own happiness.

179. Nathless . . . A contracted form of nevertheless.

199. There was a mortal . . . The reference is to St. Francis of Assisi, who, two years before his death, while contemplating in prayer on Mt. Alvernia the passion of Christ, was miraculously transformed into an image of Christ Crucified, inasmuch as the Five Wounds of the Passion were visibly imprinted on his hands, feet, and

side by Our Lord Himself, appearing as a
Seraph with six wings resplendent and aflame,
bearing the image of the Crucified. This stigma-
tization, as it is called, produced in St. Francis at
once exceeding joy and piercing pain.

PARAGRAPH V.

Line 1. Hark to those sounds . . . The Choirs
of Angelicals, one after another, sing the praises
of God, harmoniously rehearsing the whole history
of man.

6. In all His words . . . Not merely spoken
utterances, but also deeds executed; as in Scripture language the Hebrew *Dabar* and the Latin
Verbum mean both word and deed.

8. His elder race . . . The whole hierarchy of
Angels.

12. The younger son . . . Man, who unites in
his nature all things outside of God, both spiritual
and material.

18. To serve as champion . . . Man is the
crown of the visible creation destined by God to
rule the whole visible world in His stead, and to
turn it to his own service.

19. elemental war . . . War of the elements
that constitute the material universe.

22. towards the foe . . . Satan and his hosts,
who, after their ejection from heaven, were allowed to carry on a war of hatred against God

and His Elect. In this war man was to prove his
fidelity to his Maker.

33. **made up of life** . . . The Roman Breviary
has a hymn in the Office for the Dedication of a
Church, in which the heavenly Jerusalem is described as made up of living stones: —

> Coelestis urbs Jerusalem,
> Beata pacis visio,
> Quae celsa de *viventibus*
> *Saxis* ad astra tolleris,
> Sponsaeque ritu cingeris
> Mille Angelorum millibus.

> Blessed city, heavenly Salem,
> Vision dear of peace and love
> Who, of *living stones* upbuilded,
> Art the joy of heaven above,
> And with angel cohorts circled
> As a bride to earth dost move.

41. **A recreant in the fight** . . . By his dis-
obedience to God.

44. **the angry sky** . . . The anger and indig-
nation of an offended God.

45. **the tempest's din** . . . The revolt of external nature, especially animals and hurtful natural influences.

56. **dreed** . . . Suffered.

56. **age by age** . . . The 4,000 years that pre-

ceded the coming of the Redeemer, in the course
of which man's helplessness and entire dependence
on God were forcibly brought home to him.

60. **And quickened by the Almighty's breath**
. . . During the long interval between the promise
of the Redeemer and His actual coming, God did
not altogether abandon man, His disobedient son,
but gave the grace of Redemption by anticipation
to all who deserved it.

66-67. **A household . . . and a state** . . .
The founding of the Jewish nation, which God
selected as the living preparation for the advent of
the Saviour.

72. **like the rushing of the wind** . . . How
admirably the sound of the words corresponds to
their meaning!

77. **Descend ecstatic odors** . . . The figure
called Prolepsis: the epithet *ecstatic* is introduced
in advance of the odors, which are the cause of
the ecstasy.

86. **For them no twilight or eclipse** . . . The
trial of the Angels, as described in this stanza,
forms a beautiful contrast to the description in the
next few stanzas of man's trial.

93. **The morning dawned on all** . . . The
coming of the Saviour, with His light and warmth-
giving grace, is aptly likened to the rising sun.

95. **divide the precious and the base** . . .
The Elect — those who avail themselves of the

merits of Christ — are even now being gradually separated from the wicked.

99. his second birth . . . Baptism, through which man is restored to the supernatural life and to the inheritance of the sons of God.

107. The forfeit of his sins . . . By sin man had lost not only the supernatural life of the soul, which made him a perfect image and likeness of God, but had lost as well all the preternatural gifts, that is, privileges bestowed on man, which elevated him above his own nature to a state similar to that of the Angels. These privileges, chief among them immortality of the body, were forfeited by sin, and not restored by Redemption.

109. The penance-fire . . . Purgatory, a middle state between Heaven and Hell, where departed souls are detained because of their being still burdened either with unforgiven venial sins, or with an uncancelled debt of temporal punishment for their forgiven sins.

119. A sovereign febrifuge . . . A medicine to cure fever.

120. And yet withal . . . How paradoxical, yet how convincing!

133. as to be used so vilely . . . The mystery of the permission of evil: that God should have allowed Himself to be injured or damaged in His external glory by His creature's offense.

143-144. The longing for Him . . . A superb

description of the paradoxical nature of the punishment of Purgatory: the tenderest love joined
to the most bitter contrition and sorrow.

154-169. Observe the greater sweep and roll in
the verse as the fervidness of the sentiment grows.

156. By man hath come the infinite display
. . . The goodness and mercy of God, and the
greatness and superabundance of Christ's saving
grace through the Incarnation, shine forth most
brilliantly in the varied history of man.

163. Amid the garden shade . . . The garden
of Gethsemane.

166. the Law which He Himself had made
. . . "In what day soever thou shalt eat of it
(the tree of knowledge of good and evil) thou
shalt die the death." Gen. II. 17.

176-195. The foe blasphemed . . . A strong
presentation of Satan's contempt for God's recreant
son, rebellious man.

179. The frontier place . . . Where man was
to have proved his fidelity to his Maker, and to
have covered the devil with greater shame, in that
the enemy should have been overcome by the
weaker creature, "a being of flesh and blood."

202-221. O loving wisdom of Our God: . . .
The unwarranted boast which the foe had made,
as if God had reckoned ill, receives a fit reply in
the song of the Fifth Choir of Angelicals. They
tell in glowing words of God's infinite mercy,

wisdom and goodness, which found in the Incarnation a means not only of wresting fallen man
from the grasp of the sneering tyrant, but also of
elevating him to a state of perfection higher than
that from which he fell. Human nature had en-
grafted upon it the Author of grace, so that now
it lay in the power of every child of Adam to become himself a god, another Christ.

212. **God's presence** . . . Through the Incarnation and the Holy Eucharist.

214-217. **that He who smote** . . . A succinct
expression of Christ's vicarious satisfaction: Christ
in His human nature suffers death to repurchase
for man the liberty of the sons of God.

PARAGRAPH VI.

Line 5. Subvenite . . . See note on line 12 of
paragraph II.

12. **Jesu, by that shuddering dread which fell
on Thee!** Observe again, how fittingly the metre
is changed to suit the underlying sentiment.

23. **To that glorious Home** . . . This last line
of the Angel's prayer literally overflows, as in intensity of appeal, so in the number of feet, with
mention of the sight of the Most Fair.

24. **Ah!** . . . The bare exclamation after what
has gone before is more piercingly eloquent than
any words, however burning, could have been.

29. But, ere it reach them . . . How vividly
the Angel portrays the act of judgment! The
very words seethe and crackle as he tells how
the happy suffering soul is smitten by the keen
sanctity of the Crucified.

36. Take me away . . . The Soul now feels
what the Angel meant when he spoke of his approaching agony: —

> the sight of the Most Fair
> Will gladden thee, but it will pierce thee too.

And again: —

> thou wilt desire
> To slink away, and hide thee from His sight,
> And yet wilt have a longing aye to dwell
> Within the beauty of His countenance.

PARAGRAPH VII.

**Line 1. Now let the golden prison ope its
gates** . . . Purgatory is here called a golden prison,
a name which fitly designates the paradoxical state
in which the Soul is now placed.

8-19. Lord, Thou hast been our refuge . . .
A paraphrase of Psalm 89, which is a prayer for
the mercy of God, recounting the shortness and
miseries of the days of man.

22-37. Farewell . . . How subduingly tender
and affectionate the words of parting! For the
verse, see Introduction.